I0157036

Courageous Healers Publishing

45055 Ramblewood Court

La Quinta, CA 92253

www.courageoushealers.org

Ordering Information:

Quantity sales: Special discounts are available on quantity purchases by corporations, associations, and others. For details, contact the "Special Sales Department" at the address above.

30-Daily Devotional To Wholeness

30-Day Devotional

To

Wholeness

With scriptures, contemplative questions and action steps
to be taken for personal change.

By: Randy Boyd

Author of: *Healing The Man Within*

&

7-Day Challenge

30-Day Devotional to Wholeness

Table of Contents

Acceptance vs. Approval

Hebrews 13:2

"Do not neglect to show hospitality to strangers, for by this some have entertained angels without knowing it."

"And acceptance is the answer to all my problems today. When I am disturbed, it is because I find some person, place, thing, situation -- some fact of my life -- unacceptable to me. And I can find no serenity until I accept that person, place, thing, or situation as being exactly the way it is supposed to be at this moment. Nothing, absolutely nothing happens in God's world by mistake. Until I could accept my alcoholism, I could not stay sober; Unless I accept life completely on life's terms, I cannot be happy. I need to concentrate not so much on what needs to be changed in the world but as on what needs to be changed in me and my attitudes.[1]"

When I entered into recovery in 2006, I was living in denial. I denied that I had any problem. I was denying the fact that I had no part of being abused, I was just a person that had a black cloud over his head. A person who deserved to be treated poorly. After all, my parents divorced when I was just ten years old. Then, God took my father from me when he died of cancer in 1969. However, the final blow came when my stepfather began emotionally, physically, spiritually and sexually abusing me right after my father died. It must have been me. If only I had been a better son, student or athlete. If only I had been better looking and smarter; then none of this would have happened to me. I had to arrive at a place of acceptance that what happened to me had absolutely nothing to do with me.

Remember this, acceptance does not mean approval. Acceptance is not submission, it is an acknowledgment of the facts of a situation, then deciding what you're going to do about it. If we are not accepting people, places, and things, then we

---

[1] **Alcoholics Anonymous, 4th Edition p. 417**

1

are fighting them. I had to quit fighting everyone and everything. I had to come to grips with the fact that I am no less of a man by admitting that another person had abused me. The reality is, it takes a strong and courageous man to admit his weaknesses, and in doing so, he will become stronger. An oldtimer once told me, *"Randy you have the power to change the world within you."* I thought he had lost his mind. However, he was absolutely right. When I quit fighting everything and everyone and arrived at a place of acceptance, the world did change. Actually, the world didn't change, it was my perception of the world that changed, and yours can too.

- Are you still living in denial?

- Who and what are you still fighting?

- Are you willing to quit fighting everything and everyone?

- What action steps are you going to take to arrive at a place of acceptance?

Prayer: Lord, I ask that you show me what parts of my life I am living in denial. Help me to confront those areas and turn them over to you. Help me to come to the point of acceptance and quit fighting everything and everyone so that I may experience true freedom and happiness. In Jesus name – Amen.

Acts of Kindness

Colossians 3:12

"So, as those who have been chosen of God, holy and beloved, put on a heart of compassion, kindness, humility, gentleness, and patience;"

One of the things I learned early on in my recovery was to no matter what, keep my side of the street clean. This means acting with kindness when you don't really feel like it. Something I wasn't really good at, especially with my wife.

I was building a business and managing 80 employees, which meant I was wearing several hats during the day and dealt with a fair amount of stress.

My wife was building her desk as an escrow officer. Being what is known as the best escrow officer in the valley, and because she is known as a "legend" in her business, she too was busy herself. She was dealing with very demanding and entitled clients, which meant she was under a lot of stress herself.

When we would talk in the evening, and she would start telling me about her day, my response was usually something like this: "really, you have no idea what stress is about until you've sat at my desk. Trying to manage 80 people, keep work coming in, and manage hundreds of thousands of dollars. I'm sorry, but your job can't be all that hard."

Wow, really Randy. It was all about me. Well, I made my amends and so today, it's a lot different.

Early in recovery, I learned to take my troubles and worries to my sponsor or my accountability partners. That way, I could go home leaving the baggage from that day where it belonged, with God. Thus, I could be more tentative to my wife.

Today, I'm there for my wife. I genuinely want to know how HER day was. I want her to be able to lean on me when she's having it bad or is sad. I'm her husband, and I love her more than words can say, so I show her with my acts of Kindness.

Galatians 5:22-23 says *But the fruit of the Spirit is love, joy, peace, patience, kindness, goodness, faithfulness, gentleness, self-control; against such things, there is no law.*

I can't fix Cathy or take away her pain, all I can do is be there for her and love her, the ultimate act of kindness.

Are you keeping your side of the street clean regardless of the other person's actions? Are you acting with kindness? If not, - then turn the page and start today. It's never too late to start over.

- Are you acting with kindness towards your co-workers, friends, children, and spouse?

- Are you acting selfishly and not caring about how others feel?

- What are you willing to do to start acting with kindness towards others?

- What action steps are you going to take to change?

Prayer: Lord, I ask that you show me how to start treating those I interact with, with your love, joy, peace, patience, kindness, goodness, faithfulness, gentleness, and self-control. In Jesus name – Amen.

Anger

Ephesians 4:26-27

"And "don't sin by letting anger control you." Don't let the sun go down while you are still angry, for anger gives a foothold to the devil."

Growing up in a Christian home and emotionally, physically, spiritually, and sexually being abused by Christian parents, one a Deacon of the church and the other a member of the choir, left me confused and very angry. Not only was I angry at my parents and the world, but I was also angry at God. After all, isn't God supposed to be our protector?

For over thirty years, that anger fueled a hate and resentment that nearly destroyed my life. Did I have a right to be angry? Absolutely! However, I was using that anger in the wrong way. I was using it to assassinate my parent's character and turn others away from God and the church.

Genesis 50:20 says - *You intended to harm me, but God intended it all for good. He brought me to this position so I could save the lives of many people.* I am grateful for God's grace and forgiveness. Today, I have turned that bitter anger and hate into compassion and love for others that have gone through the same suffering. I know that through all of my abuse, God was always right next to me weeping and protecting me from grave harm.

I want you to know that no matter what you have been through, there is hope and healing for you. There is a better life waiting for you. Jeremiah 29:11 says - *For I know the plans I have for you, "declares the LORD," plans to prosper you and not to harm you, plans to give you hope and future.*

- Are you still harboring anger towards something or someone from your past?

- Are you now ready to release that anger and give it to God?

5

- What action steps will you take to release your anger?

Prayer: Lord, remove the anger that has me trapped and replace it with your love and give me the strength to forgive anyone that caused me pain. In Jesus name – Amen.

Belonging

1 John 4:4

"But you belong to God, my dear children. You have already won a victory over those people because the Spirit who lives in you is greater than the spirit who lives in the world."

Have you ever felt as though you do not belong here, as though you are all alone? For many years I did. I would be sitting in a stadium surrounded by thousands of people, yet I felt all alone.

I grew up in an abusive home where my voice did not matter, and my feelings were nullified. I felt as though I was the only one in the world that was being abused. The pastor of our church even told me it was just part of growing up. The shame that is attached with sexual abuse made it even worse; I was afraid to say anything out of fear that I would not be believed.

To feel like I belonged, I chased all the "things" the world tells us will make us happy. I became successful in business, surrounded myself with people I perceived to be successful and have want I wanted. But no matter how much I achieved or how much material wealth I acquired, I never really felt like I belonged. You see it was all a facade to hide my pain and fill the hole in my soul. I was afraid that if the facade came tumbling down, you'd see just how dirty, tainted, and broken I was.

Here is what I know today – I was never alone. When I look back over my life, even after my fall from grace in 1975, I was able to see everywhere God was with me. Despite my circumstances, despite my sin, despite all of the terrible conditions happening around me and despite the lie I had been listening to – I was not alone. Today, I have days where I might feel lonely, but all I have to is call out to God, and he will be

7

there for me, and he will be there forever as well.

Today I am never alone - God will not leave me.

Hebrews 13:5 - *Keep your lives free from the love of money and be content with what you   have, because God has said, "Never will I leave you; never will I forsake you."*

- Do you feel like you do not belong?
- What happened in your life to make you feel like you are alone?
- What things are you chasing in your life to feel that void?
- What action steps are you going to take to feel like you are a part of?

Prayer: Lord, when I feel all alone, blanket me with your grace and loving kindness to ward off rejection and loss of friends and family. Help me to feel your presence and trust that you are always with me. May this season of loneliness draw me closer to you. In Jesus Name –Amen.

Childlike

Matthew 19:4

"But Jesus said, "Let the little children come to me and do not hinder them, for to such belongs the kingdom of heaven."

Growing up, it is highly unlikely that any of us has escaped our childhood without facing some form of trauma. Rather, it is emotional, physical, spiritual, or sexual. We have all had our childhood issues. Some of us have been able to deal with it better than others and for the most part, have had no adverse effects as a result of whatever childhood trauma you might have faced. For others, their lives have been riddled with adverse effects.

My abuse started at an early age and continued until I was eighteen. It is my belief that God gives us the innate ability to survive no matter what the conditions. With my father on the verge of death when I was twelve years old, and my mother and stepfather being abusive and unable to parent me the way a child should be parented, I was never really allowed to be a child. From a very young age, I was being told to figure it out for myself. I had poor male role models in my life growing up, and the way I dealt with adversity was by acting like a spoiled little boy that didn't get his way. People would bully and manipulate me to get what they wanted, much like a spoiled little boy would do.

As an adult, when I felt threatened or felt like a business deal was going south, what would I do? The only thing I knew how to do. I would throw a temper tantrum or try to manipulate people into using my company or doing what I wanted. Why? Because I had an inner child in me that was scared to death, and that inner child was never given the proper tools to deal with adversity or rejection like gentlemen.

Picture this if you will – An actual child throwing the worst tantrum you have ever seen. Now give that child your credit cards, your phone, and your keys. When you lose your tenuous grip on your emotional state, your adult self becomes a passenger, and your inner child self takes the wheel. You can imagine what the outcome might be if this scenario were to be played out.

The good news is *you can change*. I found a couple of older gentlemen as mentors, and they gently and lovingly pointed out my adverse behavior and taught me how to act like a mature husband, father and contributing member of society. If I can change with God's help, I know you can.

Proverbs 22:6 says: *"Train up a child in the way he should go; even when he is old he will not depart from it."* It is important to know that if you train up your child to act like a kid when matured, then that is what he/she will do. Conversely, if you train up your child to be a responsible adult and act like a responsible adult, then they will be and act responsibly.

- Do you still have a devious inner child in you that wreaks havoc in your life?

- Are you willing to meet and help this inner child become a responsible adult?

- What are you willing to do to begin re-parenting your wounded inner child?

Prayer: Lord, I pray that you give me the patience and love to embrace my broken inner child. Give me the guidance to embrace and love. Also, teach me the ways of a mature God loving man. In Jesus name – Amen.

Dating

Colossians 3:23

"Whatever you do, work at it with all your heart, as working for the Lord, not for human masters."

Today, my wife and I have a great dating life, which has brought us closer together emotionally, spiritually, and physically. I believe it is also why we have been married now for 30-Plus years and our marriage still flourishes and is getting stronger.

Question: Are you still dating your wife?

Let's be honest, the honeymoon is long over, and your job is demanding all your time, and you can't take time off because you're trying to climb up a corporate ladder, so you and your family can have a comfortable life.

Because you're busy climbing the corporate ladder or just making a living for you and your family, your spouse is busy with the kids. Getting them off to school, picking them up from school, and getting them to and from their soccer games or dance recitals.

By the time you both get home you're exhausted. You're lucky if you get ten minutes with each other without any interruptions before you're out for the night, only to get up in the morning and repeat the dance all over again. Welcome to life.

Then one day we wake up, and the kids are all grown and out of the house. We suddenly realize that the woman/man lying in bed next to us is a complete stranger. Now don't get your feathers all ruffled, it's still the man or woman we married, we just don't know who they are anymore.

Why? Well, it's most likely because we get so caught up in the business of life that we have neglected our relationship with our spouse. We quit flirting with and dating them. The flame eventually burns into an ember and then a spark. I believe it's when we neglect the spark that our marriage can get in trouble; perhaps the grass begins looking greener on the other side.

My wife and I have gone through all of these and the spark at one point was all but extinguished. What saved us? We returned to the dating game every week.

But Randy you don't understand how busy I am. Yes, I do. I owned a very large construction company with 80 employees, my wife is a very successful escrow officer and we raised three children. So I know how life can get in the way.

Here's a challenge if you're willing: On Sunday night, sit down with your spouse and pull out your weekly calendar. Then, find a day and time that you can meet for twenty or thirty minutes for coffee with your spouse. Block out that day and time, and treat it as you would an important business meeting – DO NOT let anything take its place. Make this a weekly ritual.

Next, find one night a month to have a full-blown date night

- Maybe dinner and a movie.

These dates are for you and your spouse only. NO BUSINESS CALLS OR SOCIAL MEDIA! Your cell phone is   for emergencies only – Make this a priority!

Genesis 2:18 – *"The LORD God said, "It is not good for the man alone. I will make a helper suitable for him."*

- Do you feel like you and your spouse are drifting apart emotionally, physically and spiritually?
- What is the wedge in your marriage that is separating you from your spouse?
- What priorities are you putting in front of your spouse?
- What action steps will you take to reignite the flame of compassion with your spouse?

Prayer: Lord, work in me to shift my priority back to my spouse. My spouse deserves my full attention, love and support, none of which I have been giving her/him. I give you our relationship to mold and shape into the relationship you have meant it to be all along. My spouse is my helpmate, friend and lover, not my slave or roommate. Restore our marriage and fill me with the passion I had for her/him when we were first dating.

Death of Old Self

Romans 5:8

"But God demonstrates his own love for us in this: While we were still sinners, Christ died for us."

.

The disgrace and humiliation I had experienced as a teenager and young adult had become so engrained in me that it had become tied to my identity. When I moved out of the home at the age of eighteen, I was on a mission to prove to the world that I was not a worthless idiot and that I could be successful. The problem was I had no one to show me what it really looked like to be a husband, father and contributing member of society. The reality was, I was scared to death and lived my life in fear until I got sober in 2006.

For years, I would latch on to anybody that showed any amount of kindness and acceptance towards me. People who I thought had all the things in life that I wanted; a beautiful wife; nice home; successful business; nice cars; and all the toys one could possibly want – the things that I believed would fill the hole in my soul and make me happy. Oh don't get me wrong, all of these things make life very enjoyable, but they do not bring that true unshakable happiness and joy that I was so desperately seeking.

Unfortunately, the men I was looking up to for thirty-plus years were not the healthiest of men to be looking up to. It is true that they were successful and had achieved much in life, and yes they had all that I desired to achieve. However, they were also men of the world, selfish; self-centered; drinking; drugging; and having affairs. They say birds of a feather flock together, so it is no wonder that I became selfish; self-centered; addicted to alcohol and drugs; and had an affair – all learned behavior.

In 1975, I turned my back on God and the church. And after thirty-plus years of following the ways of the world, I had to change, do something different. Even though I had achieved everything I had set out to achieve, the hole in my soul had grown bigger and I was more miserable than ever. When I started my journey of recovery, Alcoholics Anonymous with the help of two very spiritually solid men, allowed me to question the God I grew up with and reconnect to a loving, kind, compassionate, and forgiving God as well as a great church.

Through all of my thirty-plus years of following the ways of the world, God never quit loving me. God was always with me, protecting me in ways I never knew were possible. With all that had happened to me, all that I had done, how could God ever forgive me, how could I ever forgive myself? Well, the answer is right here in Luke 5:20 – "*When Jesus saw their faith, he said, 'Friend, your sins are forgiven.'*" It can't be much clearer than that.

Who have you been looking up to in your life?

- Are they living by the ways of the world or are they living by the principles of Christ?

- Do they have only the material things that you desire but live a life of dishonesty and discontent?

- Do they have the bare minimum materially yet are happy, healthy and love life?

- Remember – birds of a feather do flock together.

Prayer: Lord, Give me Your grace and guidance in the choices I need to make and direct my thinking so that my firm resolved and final decisions will be in line with Your perfect will for my life. Thank You, Father, that Your grace is sufficient and that no matter where I go or what I do, You have promised to be with me. In Jesus name – Amen.

Disgraced

Psalms 40:14

"Let those be ashamed and humiliated together Who seek my life to destroy it; Let those be turned back and dishonored Who delight in my hurt."

I believe that sarcasm is one of the most humiliating and disgraceful acts imposed on another human being. I grew up in a house where sarcasm was a way of manipulating me into doing and believing things I really didn't want to do or believe. When and if I ever expressed how they made me feel with their sarcastic remarks, I was met with – *Come on Randy, we were just kidding!* But it was too late, the hurt had already happened. You see, words pierce the heart in a way nothing else in this world can.

While words can be the most damaging tool the enemy uses to destroy the child spirit in us, add physical abuse to the mix, and that child's spirit seeks shelter in some very dark places. The severe beatings I received with a belt by my stepfather I could endure, but when the words – *You're an idiot, and you'll never amount to anything* – were added with each crack of the belt, you feel worthless, less than and humiliated.

There are not too many things in this world that can make a boy/man feel more disgraceful than being sexually abused. As a man, I felt weak like there was something wrong with me as a man. Why was I the only one this was happening to? However, when I heard these words of my then pastor – *Randy its just part of growing up and you are not and will not be gay* – the disgrace and humiliation came pouring down over me as though a huge thundercloud had opened up its floodgates.

I carried the secret and pain of my abuse with me until I was forty-nine, no one knew about my abuse other than my wife. I turned my back on God and the church when I was eighteen and felt as though I was walking under a huge cloud of humiliation, disgrace, and shame for most of my adult life. I didn't think anyone cared about my pain, after all, I was constantly being told – *Who do you think you are, just get over it.*

Well, who am I? My name is _____, and I am a child of God, and my voice, my pain, my disgrace, and my shame do matter. Jesus does care about and love me, regardless of what I have been told by others. God does not care that I turned my back on him, he has loved me and protected me all of my life. Like the prodigal son when I turned to God for help, he was there with loving and open arms for me. Luke 15:20 say *[20] "So, he got up and went to his father. But while he was still a long way off, his father saw him and was filled with compassion for him; he ran to his son, threw his arms around him and kissed him."*

- Who in your life has disgraced or humiliated you?

- Are you willing to start the process of forgiveness for those that have hurt you?

- Are you willing to make amends to those that you have hurt?

- Remember we cannot change the past, but what we can change is the future.

Prayer: Lord, Please grant me the intercession of losing the burden of being a disgraced and shamed son/daughter. What I have gone through is severe. Even though I might feel loved and protected in my own home, let me know Heavenly

Father that you are always there to hold, nurture, affirm and protect me. I pray that your angels will surround and protect me in my times of need. In Jesus name – Amen.

Ensnared

2 Corinthians 4:4

"The god of this age has blinded the minds of unbelievers so that they cannot see the light of the gospel that displays the glory of Christ, who is the image of God."

When I turned eighteen–years old, I turned my back on the church and God, and for the next 30–plus years, I ran with the devil. You see in my eyes God had taken my father from me when I was twelve–years old when he died of cancer. Next, the man that God put in my life to be my stepfather abused me emotionally, physically, spiritually, and sexually, which is something that no father figure should ever do. The pastor of our church knew about it yet did nothing about it. And finally, my youth pastor slammed the door in my face when I needed him the most. I had fallen right into the devils snare, which lead me down a road of drugs, alcohol, and infidelity; I had become the devil's number one advocate. His plan had been executed perfectly.

However, Gods plans are far greater than the devils, and today I am Gods number one advocate and the devils number one adversary, and he is mad.

I could never understand why I was being abused and more often than not felt like I was the only one this was happening to. Why me God? What had I done to deserve this abuse? Maybe I was just a bad seed. When I was in therapy, and I would ask my therapist these questions, she would simply reply – *Randy it's none of your business.* Pretty harsh I know, but there is a lot of truth to it. I learned in recovery that either God is or He is not and there is no in between, period! You see God had a plan for my life. Jeremiah 1:5 says - *"Before I formed you in the womb I knew you before you were born I set you apart; I appointed you as a prophet to the nations."* Nothing happens in God's world by accident and everything that happened was part of God's plan for me.

Today, God and His ways protect me.

Genesis 50:20 says – *"You intended to harm me, but God intended it all for good. He brought me to this position so I could save the lives of many people."*

Do you blame God for the misfortunes in your life?

Do you feel like God is punishing you?

Do you pray to God only when you are in trouble (prayers from the foxhole)?

- Make a list of the ways you feel God has punished you.

- Was it God or man that was harming you?

- Make a list of the times you made a prayer from the foxhole, and God answered it.

- If God were punishing you, why would he answer your prayers from the foxhole?

Prayer: Loving God, I have been going through some painful memories from my childhood, which I just can't seem to get rid of. No matter how hard I try – they keep on returning to haunt me. God, please give me the strength and courage to do my part in healing these painful memories. In Jesus name – Amen.

Entrapped

2 Timothy 2:26

"Then they will come to their senses and escape from the devil's trap. For they have been held captive by him to do whatever he wants."

For 30-plus years, I was a prisoner of my past. I was entrapped in my self-loathing, self-hatred and self-doubt. Drugs and alcohol had become a way of anesthetizing the pain of my childhood trauma. However, as much as the drugs and alcohol kept me numb from the shame and pain of the past, it also kept me entrapped in the prison of being a victim.

I did not realize that as an adult, I was living at an emotional level equal to that of the teenager I was when my abuse started, and my chemical dependency kicked in. I developed survival skills and coping mechanisms that worked really well as a teenager and not so good as an adult. The problem was that no one ever taught me about the adult behaviors that I needed to survive in an adult world. I had become an egomaniac with a huge inferiority complex, not a good combination for survival in the real world.

Fortunately for me in 2006, I had a very good therapist, and two wise mentors enter my life. These men and women gently and lovingly over time, pointed out how my actions replicated that of my inner child. This inner child had been entrapped behind the prison walls of drugs, alcohol, and fear. They helped me, with much love and patience; to break down those prison walls and learn new and more mature coping skills. Thus allowing my inner child to grow and mature into the adult man I am today.

Today, I am free from the prison walls that kept me living and acting like a teenager in an adult world. Today, I am living life on life's terms, it's not always easy, but it is a whole better than living life on Randy's unrealistic terms. With a little faith and work, you too can be free from the bondage of your past.

22

Galatians 5:1 says – *"It is for freedom that Christ has set us free. Stand firm, then, and do not let yourselves be burdened again by a yoke of slavery."*

– Is there something from your past that is keeping you entrapped in behaviors that no longer serve you?

– Are you willing to replace old toxic behaviors with new healthy behaviors?

– What action steps are you willing to take to make the switch from toxic to healthy behaviors?

Prayer: Lord, at those times when I just don't feel good enough, help me to remember that You are continually working on me. May I always recognize my true worth and value especially when others put me down. You have already started a good work in my heart Lord, and it shall be completed. In Jesus name – Amen.

Forgiveness

Matthew 6:14-15

"For if you forgive others for their transgressions, your heavenly Father will also forgive you. "But if you do not forgive others, then your Father will not forgive your transgressions."

Today, forgiveness is one of my favorite topics to talk about; however, it wasn't always like that. As a survivor of abuse, I became real good at blaming all my problems on my mother and stepfather. I was harboring so much resentment, anger and hate towards them that I couldn't see the forest through the trees, it was crippling.

There are three things that people would constantly say to me, and these three things I believe can be very crippling to survivors – "you just need to forgive, forget and move on!" Every time I heard those words I just cringed, and would say – *"You have no idea what those people did to me. If what was done to me was done to you, you'd act this way and drink yourself!"* Poor pitiful me – There is no way I will ever forgive them.

Today, I can say that the true key to freedom and happiness is forgiveness. That being said, it is important to know that forgiveness is a process that takes time, how much time I cannot tell you; that depends on the depth of the harm and the willingness to do the work. The depth of harm done to me was deep, so once I started my recovery journey, it took about two years for me to forgive my mother and stepfather.

My journey to forgiveness began when I walked into the Betty Ford Center in 2006. For the first time in my life, my voice was heard, and I was listened to without judgment. My feelings were validated, something that had never happened before. I was told that I had the right to be angry with my mother, stepfather, and yes-even God. Once this part of the process was done, I was able to begin the journey of learning how to let go and forgive.

To put your mind at ease, I have listed a few things about forgiveness:

- Forgiveness does not mean reconciliation. (You are not required to allow your abuser back in your life to have a relationship with him or her).[2]

- Forgiveness is not trusting. (You need to be exceedingly careful about whom you trust).

- Forgiveness is not approving or diminishing the abuse or sin. (The sinfulness of the abuse never changes).

Until you forgive, you are still hostage to your abusers. When you do forgive, you set yourself free.

Romans 12:18-19 says *-"Do all that you can to live in peace with everyone. Dear friends, never take revenge. Leave that to the righteous anger of God."*

- Who do you still have resentment and un-forgiveness towards?
- Have you been unable to forgive yourself?
- Are you ready to experience true freedom and happiness?
- What action steps are you going to take to start your forgiveness process?

Prayer: Lord, help me to see where and who I am I holding onto resentment and un-forgiveness towards. Help me to start the process of forgiveness so I may experience the freedom and happiness you desire me to have. I don't know how to forgive, but I know that through you all things are possible. **In Jesus Name – Amen.**

Gentleness

Philippians 4:5

"Let your gentleness be evident to all. The Lord is near."

I don't believe that I was born evil, wicked or mean. In fact, I believe I was born a loving, caring, compassionate and kind human being. However, I do believe that my behaviors, in part, are a result of those behaviors that were modeled to me. I believe most people if they were to be truly honest about it, would say the same thing.

I believe that our behaviors are all learned behaviors that have been passed down from generation to generation. So then does that make our behaviors right?

When my father passed away, my positive male role model was gone, and the one that would take his place was everything but a good role model. Yes, he took my brother and I in, but I believe that was only because we were attached to my mother.

This is not intended to throw my mother and stepfather under the bus. They both had their very deeply rooted unresolved issues. However, this is my personal truth.

My stepfather was an extremely tormented man, which meant that he was very angry and violent. He was also the one that modeled to me how to treat a woman and a wife, which was with disrespect and disregard for their feelings. And my mother modeled to me how women were supposed to be submissive to their husband no matter what.

When I first met Cathy, and for the first 15 years, I treated her like a queen. But then my unresolved childhood trauma reared its ugly head. Cathy went from being my queen to be my servant. I began trying to change her, and I began emotionally abusing her, calling her names and using language I can only describe as very emotionally damaging. After all, isn't that how women are supposed to be treated? That's what was ultimately modeled to me after all. The answer is unequivocally NO! I hated myself for treating Cathy like a servant girl. Truth be told, this is really hard for me to put out there.

When I entered recovery, this was one of the first areas of my life, second only to my abuse that I worked on. I had two older and wiser male mentors (sponsors) that begin helping me to transform into the man and husband I wanted to be. It has taken work, a lot of work, but today I have returned to being that loving, caring, compassionate and kind husband God has called me to be. Cathy is my queen, and I treat her as such. Am I perfect? Absolutely not. However, I no longer use language that is damaging or belittles Cathy. Today, I treat her with the respect and gentleness a queen deserves. No women, wife or daughter, deserves to be treated like anything less than a queen.

Remember, your wife didn't start out hardened and sturdy; you likely made her that way. I know I did. Remember, harshness will close her spirit and gentleness will do otherwise.

Proverbs 16:24-*"Pleasant words are as a honeycomb, sweet to the soul, and health to the bones."*

- Has your wife/spouse developed a hardened heart towards you over time?

- Do you live in a world where the man's the man?

- Do you believe that being the man of the house gives you the right to mistreat your wife and children?

- How is that working for you?

- What action steps are you going to take to change?

Prayer: Lord, I ask that you show me how to treat my spouse and children like the king/queen, princesses, and princes that they are. Let me always be reminded to love them like Christ loved the church. In Jesus name – Amen.

God's Authority Not Mine

Colossians 3:18-19

"Wives, submit yourselves to your husbands, as is fitting in the Lord. Husbands, love your wives and do not be harsh with them."

We started out like most couples. We dated, worshiped the ground each other walked on and did whatever we thought would make each other happy.

Then we got married and started to build a life together. Both of us had great full-time jobs and we combined our finances. After all, we are married, and we both believed and still do believe our finances do not need to be separated.

Then along came children and all the responsibilities that came with them. Along with all these changes, I gradually became more controlling. After all, I am the man of house. Therefore, it's my job to take control of our marriage. The problem was, I was doing it under my authority with absolutely no authority or direction from God.

Slowly, Cathy withdrew from me. She couldn't wait for me to go on one of my week-long excursions and dreaded the day I returned.

As I look back on it, I can't blame her; I wouldn't have wanted me around either. I was controlling, manipulating, demanding, and miserable.

Yes, the bible tells us in Ephesians 5:22 - *"Wives, submit yourselves to your own husbands as you do to the Lord."* However, there is a prerequisite. Ephesians 5:25 says - *"Husbands, love your wives, just as Christ loved the church and gave himself up for her."*

Today, I love Cathy as described in Ephesians 5:25 and therefore, she loves me as she does the Lord.

We are to love and respect each other equally.

Are we perfect, absolutely not? Today, I honor and respect Cathy, and therefore, she honors and respects me, all because today I operate under the direction and authority of God.

- Whose authority are you operating under?

- Husbands, do you love your wife as Christ loved the church?

- Wives, do you submit yourselves to your husband as you do the Lord?

- What action steps are you going to take to come under and operate under God's authority, not your own?

Prayer: Lord, I thank you for the wonderful spouse you have gifted me with. Father, I am sorry if I have mistreated or abused my spouse in any way by operating under my authority and not yours. Please chisel, mold and shape me into the spouse you have created me to be so I may better serve and love you. In doing so, I will be able to better serve and love my spouse. In Jesus name – Amen.

GUILT

Isaiah 43:25

"I--yes, I alone--will blot out your sins for my own sake and will never think of them again."

Guilt is defined as – *a bad feeling caused by knowing or thinking that you have done something bad or wrong.*

I'm sure we have all been and/or felt guilty about something we have done in the past. The good thing about guilt is that it can be remedied rather quickly with a proper amends.

Before I entered into recovery, my life was riddled with guilt. I even felt guilty about my abuse; that in some way, I was responsible for it. If only I had been more obedient, a better student, better athlete, or better-looking, maybe I would not have been abused. The reality is, in no way was it my fault for any of my abuse, therefore, I had no reason to feel guilty.

Then as I got older, the underlying residual of my abuse manifested itself in the form of anger and rage. I justified my actions by saying *"if you had been through what I had as a child you'd be angry as well."* When I had an affair in 2004, I blamed it on my wife saying, *"If she was only more loving, I would not have left her."* However, once the effects of the alcohol I would drink to mask my pain would wear off, I would be overwhelmed with guilt – legitimate guilt.

The good thing about guilt is that it is telling our conscious mind that our *"actions and behaviors"* are wrong. Therefore, we can quickly and easily remedy our guilt by making amends to those we have harmed. Luke 6:31 says *"To do unto others as you would have do to you."*

The act of making an amends includes first making an apology to the person we have caused harm or done wrong to, without excuses. Then we work on changing our behavior as not to repeat the same hurtful behavior. My wife was tired of hearing my apologies only to have me repeat the same harmful behavior a week later. She was tired of my empty words – she wanted to see *action*.

I was told to not ask for forgiveness as that required action on the other person's part. It was up to them if they wanted to forgive me. If I were to ask for their forgiveness and they denied that request, it would likely send another wave of guilt over me. Once you have made your amends, your part is done.

Matthew 5:23-24 says *"So if you are presenting a sacrifice at the altar in the Temple and you suddenly remember that someone has something against you, leave your sacrifice there at the altar. Go and be reconciled to that person. Then come and offer your sacrifice to God."*

– Are you still carrying guilt from past harms or hurts you have caused others?

– Are you ready to have that guilt removed from your life?

– What actions steps will you take relieve your guilt?

Prayer: Heavenly Father, I come to you asking you to forgive me for holding onto the sin that you have already forgiven. I pray for the courage to promptly make my amends to_____, and I pray you remove this guilt, shame, and condemnation that is within my heart and mind concerning _____.

I Can't Change Her

Proverbs 31:10

"Who can find a virtuous and capable wife? She is more precious than rubies."

Cathy's physical beauty is what attracted my eyes to her, and it was her gentle and loving spirit that I fell in love with.

We dated, had lots of fun, became great friends, and in doing so, we fell deeper in love with each other. I couldn't believe how much I trusted Cathy, something I had a hard time doing before.

Finally, I had found everything in a woman a man could ask for - beauty; friendship; companionship; trustworthy; and a great lover. A match specially made in heaven.

After we got married, settled into a regular routine and when the honeymoon was over, things began to change. You see, I still had this issue of unresolved childhood trauma in my life, and slowly, its effects started rearing its ugly head.

All of a sudden, the woman I fell in love with and married seemed different. Suddenly, she didn't seem as fun, as physically attractive or trustworthy. So I began the impossible task of trying to change Cathy into something she wasn't, but in fact, she was in reality so much more.

Between my unresolved childhood issues and my drug and alcohol use, there was nothing Cathy could have done that would have made me happy. You see, Cathy had not changed; it was me that was changing.

Over time, Cathy became hardened to me. She couldn't wait for me to leave on one of my weeklong excursions so she could have some peace, at least for a short period. Then there was the fact she dreaded me coming home.

I married Cathy because she was everything I could have asked for in a wife, and today, she still has every one of the qualities I married her for and have added more.

In trying to change her into some fantasy women, I changed her all right, but not into my fantasy women. She became hardened and distanced from me.

We do not have the power to change anyone; only God has that much power. Twelve years ago when Cathy and I began our recovery journey, God started slowly working and molding each of us into the husband and wife and the people we were meant to be.

When I finally cut the strings that I had used to tie Cathy's wing and let her fly free, she began to grow and blossom. Today, she is so much more than I could have ever asked for. The only part I played in all of it was setting her free to become the woman God intended her to be. Of course, I have done my own changing and growing as well.

Only God has the power to change a person, and last time I checked, my name was Randy - not Jesus.

Proverbs 5:18 – *"May your fountain be blessed, and may you rejoice in the wife of your youth."*

- Do you rejoice in the wife of your youth and why you married her?

- Are you trying to change and/or mold your wife into what you think she should be?

- Do you have unresolved childhood issues that are putting a wedge between you and your wife?

- Who really changed, your spouse or yourself?

- What action steps are you willing to take to repair your marriage?

Prayer: Lord, I ask that you give me the courage and strength to examine myself. Show me how my actions and behaviors might have caused my wife to become hardened and bitter towards me. Give me the strength and courage to work on myself, and I ask that if it's your will that you would restore our marriage to a God-centered and loved marriage as you intended it to be from the beginning of time, help us realize it. In Jesus name – Amen.

I Love My Wife

Ephesians 5:22

"For wives, this means submit to your husbands as to the Lord."

When I married Cathy 30-plus years ago, I made a vow to stay married to her till death do us part. That hopefully is a very long time. However, in the lifetime of a marriage, there are going to be seasons of joy, light, dark, pain, doubt, and mistrust. It's called life. The question I have for you is this – is your love for your spouse strong enough to withstand all these seasons?

Cathy Boyd and I have gone through some very dark times in our years together. The catalyst of our marriage has been the fact that we have both chosen love over hate. Have we always been "in love" with each other? Absolutely not. Have we always liked each other? Absolutely not, but we have always had a deep love for each other. The only reason we are still married is because of this deep love that we have for each other, and that love keeps growing stronger. Don't get me wrong; we still have our issues to work on. We are a work in progress.

When I wake up in the morning, I make a conscious choice to love Cathy. Not only do I make the choice, I manifest that choice. I start by praying for her every morning. Then, I bring her coffee and breakfast in bed while she's reading her devotional. My actions and language throughout the day say, "I love you, Cathy."

For those of you that are thinking, "That's pretty codependent Randy," let's talk about that. I can understand why some of you would think this way. There's a fine line between being codependent and being loving. Ask yourself this one question - "What's my motive?" If you're performing these acts of love because you want something in return, are approval seeking, or are trying to make up for bad behavior, then you are codependent. On the other hand, if you are performing these acts of love out of the pure love of your heart, then you're on the right track.

Are you treating your spouse with love, even in your dark moments? Remember love conquers all!

I started this devotional with Ephesians 5:22 – *"For wives, this means submit to your husbands as to the Lord."*

Husbands, there is a pre-requisite to this verse – Ephesians 5:25 – *"For husbands, this means love your wives, just as Christ loved the church. He gave up his life for her."*

We are instructed to love our wives as Christ "Loved the Church." We can't expect our wives to love us and to submit to us if we are disrespecting them and not loving them as Christ loves the church. When I started loving my wife as Christ loved the church, my wife starting loving, respecting, and submitting to me as she is instructed to do in the bible.

- Do you experience periods of disliking and falling in out of love with your spouse?

- Husbands, do you truly love your wife as Christ loved the church?

- Wives, are you loving and submitting yourself to your husband as the bible instructs you to do?

- What action steps are you going to take to do as instructed in Ephesians 5:22 & 25?

- Prayer for HIM: Lord, help me to see where I do not love my wife as Christ loved the church and help me become the husband I am instructed to be that my wife may submit to me as instructed in the bible. In Jesus name – Amen.

- Prayer for HER: Lord, help me to see where I am not submitting to my husband who is loving me as Christ loved the church and help me become the wife I am instructed to be that my husband may continue to love me as instructed in the bible. In Jesus name – Amen.

I Need Her

Psalm 61:2

"From the ends of the earth, I cry to you for help when my heart is overwhelmed."

All right, men, there are times that we have to be strong and tough. In fact, our wives and family admired that in us when used and displayed appropriately. However, there is a more important emotion/feeling that our wives need to see in us, vulnerability.

Yes, you read it right, and in case you didn't see it the first time, here it is again - being vulnerable.

How often have you come home from a rough day at work, walked in the house, go directly to your favorite chair, turned the TV on and began to sulk over your day? Then when your wife comes to you and asks "what's wrong", you answer with an abrupt "NOTHING." Her response is often something like, okay then...

As time passes, you wonder why your wife is withdrawn and unaffectionate. Look in the mirror, and that's your answer. It's not your fault; you are only repeating the behavior that was displayed to you by your father, which was displayed to him by his father, and so on. It's okay, you can change.

I had to learn to become vulnerable with my wife. I know what you're saying; *I don't want to burden her with my issues.* Guess what, even if no words are said, your wife feels and goes through everything you are feeling and going through. Wouldn't it be much easier on both of you if you could talk about what was going on in your lives, after all, you are married – one in God's eyes?

Believe me, it was hard for me to start asking for my needs to be met. Hard to be vulnerable with anybody let alone my wife. The fact is gentlemen we do have needs and desires that need to be met. Sometimes, I just need to ask Cathy to sit and listen to me.

Sometimes, I have to ask for physical desires to be met. And sometimes, I'm given a loving *no* answer with an explanation why, and that I can accept. It's certainly a lot better than sulking or going to sleep upset and my wife having no idea why.

Start slowly with easy conversations. Make sure both of you have had a chance to relax. Then simply approach your wife and ask her if you can talk to her about your day and something that might be bothering you. Tell her you just need to be heard. If you're not looking for feedback, tell her that upfront. It's a process that takes time. Just trust the process.

If you really want a challenge, when you get home tonight and when she's relaxed, walk up behind her, wrap your arms around her, kiss her on the neck, and tell her you love and need her in your life. Likely, she will melt in your arms.

Even if you don't think she needs to hear this, just do it, she does need to hear it.

Remember men, it is a weak man that hides his vulnerabilities and pain. In my eyes, only a man that exposes his vulnerabilities and pain (to the right people) is truly strong and courageous.

Genesis 2:18 - *Then the LORD God said, "It is not good for the man to be alone. I will make a helper who is just right for him."*

- What is keeping you from being vulnerable with your spouse?

- Do you feel you have to bear the weight of your family's burdens on your shoulders?

- Do you believe your spouse is feeling your pain even if you don't share it?

- Who told you that you had to figure things out yourself without the input of your spouse?

Prayer: Lord, I ask that you show me how to become vulnerable with my spouse. Help me to be honest with my spouse about how I am feeling and my struggles. Lord, you gave me a helpmate that is perfect for me. I realize not trusting him/her is not trusting You. In Jesus name – Amen.

Listen When He or She Speaks

Psalm 141:4

"Set guard over my mouth, O Lord; keep watch over the door of my lips."

How often do we really listen to what others, especially our spouses, are saying to us? I believe we can all agree that we all listen to what is being said to us, but do we really *hear* what is being said? There is a difference.

When your spouse, children or a friend needs to talk with you, what are you doing in the conversation? Are you one hundred percent focused on them or are you playing on your phone/computer? Do you have all of your attention focused on the football game that's on the TV? Do you occasionally look up with a nod of the head and an uh-ha?

When was the last time, if ever, that you were really heard? Was the person listening to you more focused on their computer, cell phone or what was on the TV? How did it make you feel when you were not being heard? Well, we cannot change the past, but we can certainly change the future.

Why listen? It communicates honor, love, and acceptance – It is a sacrificial gift to another – It diffuses tension and disarms defenses – It gives time for Holy Spirit's wisdom, discernment and it enables us to choose the best questions that reveal what God is doing in *their* lives.

Cathy and I had to learn how to really sit and listen to each other, especially with our busy lives. It takes some work, but it's worth it. For Cathy and I, it has made a difference in our relationship.

Listen when he/she speaks, not because you have to, but because the person you cherish is sharing his/her heart with you.

Here is a guideline for becoming a good listener:

- If you need to talk, let your spouse know that you need their full attention. If they are in the middle of something, let them finish it, if not, they will likely not be able to concentrate on what is being said.

- Find a quiet place where there are no distractions – that means no TV, cell phone or computer. Leave them in the other room.

- Make sure you are looking at each other not away from each other.

- If you're the one listening, your job is to listen intuitively for voice changes and body language. This will help you develop powerful questions.

- The listener is not to try to fix or tell the one talking what to do only ask important questions – this empowers the person talking to come up with their own conclusions.

- Be sure to ask the one talking what you can do to help them. Remember they are the experts on their own life, not you.

"There is a time for everything, a time to be silent and a time to speak."
Eccl 3:17

Prayer: Lord, help me to learn how to not only listen but to hear what my spouse is really trying to tell me. Help me to hear her pain and joy. Help me to not only want to fix, but also be there for my spouse. Help me to listen as Jesus listens. In Jesus name - Amen.

Never Bring Up The Past

1 Peter 5:5

"God resists the proud but gives grace to the humble."

In our thirty–plus years of being married, my wife and I have had plenty of disagreements. Pre-recovery, I am sure there were times that we each brought up something that the other person had done in the past. But honestly, we are ten-plus years removed from those times and I truly can't remember if we did. Actually, most of the disagreements were a result of my wounded inner child and what happened to me as a child, so it was pretty hard to throw things in my wife's face.

What we have to remember is that the past is the past and bringing it up again, throwing it in our spouses face, only causes more pain. In reality, it only serves to cause the person putting it out there to relive the trauma and pain from the past. It keeps you trapped in a prison of anger and resentment and serves absolutely no good purpose.

Believe me, my wife has plenty of things that she could hold against me and throw in my face, such as the affair that happened ten-plus years ago. However, she knows that throwing it in my face in the middle of a disagreement will only exasperate the situation. My wife has fully forgiven me for the affair, however, that does not mean she doesn't have some residual pain. When that pain does come up, it is my job as her husband to sit down and listen to her and validate that pain, which is why she never throws it in my face in the middle of a disagreement.

Our pasts happened in the past, so why would you want to throw the past into the middle of a disagreement that is happening in the now. You CANNOT change the past, it's done and over with. If you are still struggling with something your spouse has done to you in the past, find a good mentor, sponsor, therapist, or pastor and talk to them about it. Most likely, the problem has more to do with you than your partner or spouse.

I can honestly say that today when Cathy and I are having a disagreement the past is *never* brought up. Sometimes it's hard enough working through the issue at hand. Throwing a past wrong in the mix will only make matters worse.

Ephesians 4:32 says — *"Be kind and compassionate to one another, forgiving each other, just as in Christ God forgave you."*

- Are you still holding onto something your spouse did that hurt you years ago?

- Have you acknowledged and validated any pain you might have caused your spouse?

- Are you willing to forgive your spouse for any past harm inflicted upon you?

Prayer: Lord, help me to forgive any harm that my spouse has caused me. Please heal those open wounds and help us to grow closer together through the healing process. In Jesus name – Amen.

No Secrets

Luke 8:17

"For there is nothing hidden that will not be disclosed and nothing concealed that will not be known or brought out into the open."

In my humble opinion, one sure way that can lead to the failure of marriage is keeping secrets. Remember, what's hidden in the darkness will eventually come to the light.

Pre-recovery, I had lots of secrets and those secrets often kept me up at night thinking about what would happen if my wife were to find out. Eventually, my wife did find out about my secrets and when she did, the results were never good.

There is something about a woman's intuition that should never be challenged. When I had an affair in 2004, every time I would hang up the phone with the other woman or send an email to her, my wife inevitably would know. Within a minute, she would call me and say - you just called her or you just emailed her, why?

I would keep all of my work problems and stresses to myself. I didn't want my wife to worry about them – they were my problems. Then when she wasn't close to me because I isolated myself, I wondered what was wrong with her. Here's the deal, everything we go through, deal with and feel, our spouses are going through it, dealing with it, or feeling it as well. How? By osmosis.

Yes, there are some things I talked about with other men, and my wife also discussed with other women, and that's only so we can get a better perspective on our thinking. That way we can go home and be a more loving and attentive husband/wife.

My wife is my best friend, confidant, and accountability partner. We've been married for 33 years, and she knows me better than anybody. We talk to each other about a lot of things. How our day was, our fears, our struggles, our joys and our victories.

Yes, when I first started getting honest with my wife, it was painful, both for her and myself. The rewards however, far outweigh the pain we have endured, and both of us have grown closer emotionally, spiritually and physically.

James 5:16 says – *"Therefore confess your sins to each other and pray for each other so that you may be healed. The prayer of a righteous person is powerful and effective."*

- Are you still keeping secrets from your spouse?

- Are you free to share your feelings, pain, hurts, joy, and victories with your spouse?

- What action steps are you going to take to bring your secrets into the light?

Prayer: Lord, there are secrets from my past that I am holding on to out of fear of being seen as weal or a fraud. Father, I ask that you would bring the right person into my life to reveal these secrets to. I pray that you would give me the courage and strength to release these secrets so I may be a better husband/wife and we may grow closer emotionally, spiritually and physically. In Jesus name – Amen.

Protect Yourself

Ephesians 5: 11-12

"Do not participate in the unfruitful deeds of darkness, but instead even expose them; for it is disgraceful even to speak of the things which are done by them in secret."

Before I go any further, I want to say that I debated with God and myself if I should write on this subject. However, it is too important of a topic not to. Countless men, women and yes-even pastors struggle with it. It has likely destroyed as many marriages as an actual physical affair.

By nature and the way God created us, when a beautiful woman or man walks by us certain hormones kick in. If we allow those hormones to take control of our mind, we fall into the temptation trap, which as married men/women, we don't need to visit. Like I was told by my therapist, the temptation will present itself and the thoughts will come, we just don't have to act on them.

I like the way my pastor said it. If I'm walking down the street and a beautiful woman/man is walking towards me, I look to God saying, you sure did a great job on that one Lord. Then I keep walking straight ahead without turning my head to look at her/him again.

So you say: Randy, I'm not having a physical affair. I sit in the privacy of my home and watch porn. Who can that be hurting?

Let me ask you a couple of questions:

1.) Would you be watching porn if your spouse were in the room with you?

2.) What would happen if your spouse walked in on you?

3.) What would happen if your child walked in on you?

46

The reality is this; Women/men in pornography are paid actresses/actors, getting thousands of dollars to perform in ways that are not reality. So if we are watching porn and then have the expectation that our spouse should perform the same way, we are setting ourselves up for disappointment.

Proverbs 5:18-19 says – *"May your fountain be blessed, and may you rejoice in the wife of your youth. A loving doe, a graceful deer – may her breasts satisfy you always, may you ever be intoxicated with her love."*

This is a scripture that I live by today and by doing so my love for my wife of thirty-plus years has been reignited in ways I never imagined.

- Are you still keeping secrets from your spouse?

- Are you still allowing the temptation of lust into your life?

- What action steps are you taking to protect yourself against an enticement that can destroy your marriage and quite possibly your career?

Prayer: Lord, I know that no one can win the war against sexual sins without your help. I come to you in need, and ask You to take every sexual sin I have ever committed and take it to the cross for salvation. Jesus my mind and body have strong cravings I cannot control. Lord, help me to remain clean and safe. Jesus, help me to keep focused on your love for me when temptation passes my way In Jesus name – Amen.

Self-Doubt

Corinthians 12:9

"Each time he said, "My grace is all you need. My power works best in weakness." So now I am glad to boast about my weaknesses so that the power of Christ can work through me."

I believe we all deal with self-doubt at some time in our lives, if not every day. It often starts when we are in school competing in sports or for that one special girl/boy. The thoughts of: *Am I good enough – will I make the team, or will he/she go to the prom with me* – creeps into our minds. For some, that self-doubt is what pushes them to succeed, and for others, self-doubt keeps them frozen in fear and therefore rarely if ever, achieve their dreams and calling in life.

For abuse survivors, it can be extremely crippling. We grow up in homes where our parents are constantly putting us down, telling us we will never amount to anything, and our voices are silenced by constant put-downs. It seems as though we can never do anything right. Then we carry that self-doubt into our everyday life. First, we carry it into school when we try out for sports or when asking that special one to the prom. Then, we carry it into our marriages and places of employment. In a sense, we set ourselves up for failure because our self-doubt is manifested through our actions and voices.

I have always been very successful in life, and for that, I am grateful. However, behind my success, I was operating in a tremendous amount of fear and self-doubt, often crippling me from moving forward. Once I entered into recovery, I realized how much my self-doubt had kept me from becoming all that God wanted me to become.

The only way I was able to overcome my self-doubt was to bring it into the light. I had two phenomenal mentors that helped me to overcome my self-doubt. They would sit and talk with me about my fears and then remind me that I do have a voice and I deserve to be heard. They walked with me and guided me through some of my greatest fears and self-doubt. They believed in me and loved me when I could not believe in or love myself.

Today, my self-doubt still rears its ugly head from time to time, especially when it comes to public speaking and book promotion. However, I not only have the tools that my mentors gave me, but I also have the word of God to lean on. I have a God that gives me hope and a future, a God that directs all my thoughts and actions. *What, then, shall we say in response to these things? If God is for us, who can be against us?* (Romans 8:31)

- Are you still battling self-doubt?

- Is that self- doubt keeping you from accomplishing your calling and dreams?

- Who's telling you the lies that keep you frozen in self-doubt?

- What action steps are you going to take to turn your self-doubt into self-confidence?

Prayer: Lord, I pray that you reveal to me all the areas that self-doubt is keeping me frozen in fear, and hindering me from accomplishing my calling and dreams. Father, I pray that you put the mentor(s) in my life to help through this process and become the confident man/woman of God that you want me to be. In Jesus name – Amen.

SHAME

Hebrews 12:2

"Fixing our eyes on Jesus, the author and perfecter of faith, who for the joy set before Him endured the cross, despising the shame, and has sat down at the right hand of the throne of God."

John Bradshaw, the leading authority on shame, describes shame this way – *the feeling of being flawed and diminished and never measuring up,* and Dr. Brene Brown says shame is the – *intensely painful feeling that we are unworthy of love and belonging. It is a fear of disconnection.*

I cannot say with certainty that we have all felt a sense of shame at some point in our life. However, a fair amount of you reading this probably has, I certainly have. In fact, the shame I had was so deeply rooted in the fiber of my being, it felt at times as though I was wearing a shame suit that flashed like a neon sign and smelled rancid.

You see because of the abuse I endured as a teenager, I just knew that if I removed any part of the façades I was wearing; success, money; beautiful home; beautiful wife and so on, you would see how dirty and tainted I was inside and would want nothing to do with me. Behind the façade, I had a very low self-esteem, I felt worthless, disgusting, dirty, and tainted, all lies that I had believed for far too long. The only way I could neutralize my shame was with drugs and alcohol. Eventually, that even quit working.

That was then, and today, I celebrate victory over shame – Psalms 22:5 says – *"To you, they cried and were rescued; in you, they trusted and were not put to shame."*

God does not want us to carry the shame from our past with us. When I finally surrendered, got on my knees and asked God for his help, slowly and with a lot of work on my part and with God by my side, He started removing my shame. I won't say that it is all been removed – I'm a work in progress. However today when I feel a shame attack coming on, I know where it's coming from – my past which means it is coming from Satan and not God.

Isaiah 54:4 says –*"Fear not, for you will not be put to shame; And do not feel humiliated, for you will not be disgraced; But you will forget the shame of your youth...."*

- Are you still burdened with the shame from your past hurts?

- Are you now willing to give God all your shame and let him replace it with his love for you?

- Now make a list of all the lies you have been telling yourself about whom you are as a result of the shame you have been burdened with, and give it to God to handle.

Prayer: Lord, there are dark places in my being. There are memories, circumstances, and scars that are unspeakable to me as I come before you. Heal my broken pieces Dear God, and help me to feel wholeness. Bring me into the light with you God and let me feel my fullness of being a child of God. In Jesus name – Amen.

The Authentic Self

Ephesians 4:22-24

"You were taught, with regard to your former way of life, to put off your old self, which is being corrupted by its deceitful desires; to be made new in the attitude of your minds; and to put on the new self, created to be like God in true righteousness and holiness."

One of the scariest parts of my recovery journey has been finding my authentic self, the person God intended me to be. However, I received a lot of payoff from our society for being inauthentic. I grew up learning how to pretend to be what I thought other people wanted me to be. I was taught that I received love and approval from others based on how well I conformed to what others wanted from me. The price tag for that kind of approval is far too high. I gave up my sense of self-worth when I changed who I was to get someone else's approval.

A lot of the trouble for men in particular (and especially for male survivors of sexual abuse) comes from feeling that they have to measure up to gender norms. I couldn't admit to being scared, vulnerable, or sad because that wasn't manly. I had built up a façade of being manly since the abuse started when I was twelve, hiding behind the numbing effects of drugs and alcohol. Inauthenticity can be obvious, or it can be subtle, but either way, it costs us our self-worth and happiness.

As I grew older I hid behind my success. You see as long as everything looked well on the outside, then everything on the inside must be good – wrong! Yes, I had a beautiful wife and family (and still do), beautiful home, drove nice cars, and had built a very successful construction company. If you looked at my life on the outside, it appeared as though I had it all together. According to the societal rules for men, I was a huge success. Then why was I still in so much emotional pain? Because I was not being true to myself, my authentic self. Then again, how could I if I did not know what that was supposed to look like? You see I was living my life according to how my parents told me I was supposed to be living it. I was doing what I was told to do by my parents. I was never allowed to be a child, never allowed to discover what I wanted to be. I was an unauthentic robot. Once I entered into recovery and turned my will and my life over to the care of God and did the necessary work, my authentic self started to reveal himself to me.

If you are willing, the person that you dream of being, the person who you know you are inside, is the man God and recovery will reveal to you. Learning to love yourself, to listen to your heart and to follow the voice that leads you to joy, is the reward of recovery.

There is a wonderful life out there. Survivors are already closer to it than most people because there comes a point when the coping tools of the regular world will not cut it for our pain. That is great news. When the coping skills fail, it's time to start looking for a deeper way to live a happy life. I'm not saying it's easy. I'm saying it's worth it. You're worth it, and you can do it.

- Are you still living an unauthentic life?

- Are you successful in life yet still feeling empty inside?

- Are you willing to lay down your ego-mask and let God start revealing your authentic self to you?

- What action steps are you going to take to change?

Prayer: Lord, I ask that you show me the ways that I am being unauthentic. Give me the strength and courage to lay down my ego mask. Reveal to me the authentic person that you intended me to be and mold me into that person. In Jesus name – Amen

Understood

Psalms 27:10

"Even if my father and mother abandon me, the LORD will hold me close."

Growing up and even into my adult years, I never felt like I was understood. At home, as a child and teenager, every time I tried to talk about my feelings, I was always met with a remark such as – oh Randy, it's not that big of a deal; who do you think you are; get over it, or you're exaggerating. Worse yet, I was often met with a physical beating or restriction when I would talk about how I felt.

However, there was a period that I felt people did understand me – like when I was a part of the youth group at church. But over time, I began feeling misunderstood there as well. Like I didn't fit in. Looking back on it now, it was as though they all knew that I was sexually abused and they just tolerated me. I didn't even feel safe in church. Well, I'm not safe or understood at home and now the one place I'm supposed to feel safe and understood is no longer safe for me.

Today, I understand why I might have been so misunderstood as a kid and even as an adult. I was shouldering a deep dark secret all by myself. I feared telling anyone about my abuse for a multitude of reasons. So instead, my actions and behaviors were such that I didn't understand them, so how could I expect anyone else too?

When I got into recovery and surrounded myself with people that had my best interest in mind, people that truly understood me and the pain I had been shouldering for thirty-plus years, I began understanding myself and therefore was able to change my behavior and beliefs about who I was.

Jeremiah 33:3 says – *"Call to me, and I will answer you and tell you great and unsearchable things you do not know."*

In reality, it was only after I dropped to my knees six months into my recovery and surrendered to God, that He started revealing things to me. Things that gave me the deep understanding I had been searching for in my life. God always understood me, and in his time, he revealed the things I needed to know to heal the deepest wounds of my soul.

Today I have a loving family, church family and recovery family that not only understand me but also believe in me and surround me.

Romans 15:7 says – *"Receive one another, then, just as Christ also received you, to God's glory."*

- Do you feel as though no one understands you?

- Make a list of the ways you feel misunderstood.

- Make a list of people in your life that you believe understand you.

- Now ask one of those people that understand you to sit down with you and listen to the ways you feel misunderstood.

Prayer: Lord, I thank you for the gift of life and the wonderful people I have met along this journey. Some of them inspire me, challenge me, stretch me, love me and encourage me. All of them have helped me realize how meaningful and beautiful my life is. In Jesus name – Amen.

Unity

Romans 14:19

"So then we pursue the things which make for peace and the building up of one another."

Let's face it; life is not all a bed of roses. If it were, what fun would it be? Rather, if we want to admit it or not, we all have faced hard times, my wife and I sure have. Pre-recovery on the surface, we acted like we were united in those hard times. The reality is that there were countless times that I wanted just to walk away, no runaway and hide on the beach under the boardwalk. Today, I thank God I never acted on those feelings, and if truth be told, it was only because of the love for my children and wife that I didn't. I've said countless times that my wife was an angel placed in my life by God, and that's because only God knew what it was going to take for me to grow and change – someone the exact opposite of me.

I factually know that my behaviors and actions pre-recovery exhausted Cathy. I know that there were times she could not wait for me to leave on one of my week-long excursions, and I know that there were times she was not looking forward to me returning from those trips. Today, I can honestly say that I don't blame her. However, through it all she remained true to her marriage vows and to some extent, it was only by a thread, we remained united through those hard times.

After the affair, my wife and I were both determined to fix our marriage at whatever cost. This meant that I had to let her talk about how me having an affair hurt her, and the only thing I could do was listen to her pain and validate her feelings. The journey was painful for both of us, and for probably the first time in our marriage, we were truly united with each other to the core of our being.

In 2007, a year into my recovery, I laid in the ICU unit on life support in a coma for three weeks. I was in the hospital for a total of six weeks and my recovery lasted for about three months. While in the hospital, my wife only left my bedside to go to work, which was wearing on her. When they transferred me to UCLA, she came crying to me saying she was exhausted and didn't see how she could drive to UCLA every day. So, we jointly decided that she was going to take a leave of absence from work so she could be with me every day.

Once I was released from UCLA, and during my recovery time, my wife and I had to travel to UCLA on a weekly basis. It was during this time that we started growing closer together, becoming more united than ever before. We took what could have been a time of separation and turned it into a time of uniting and growing closer together.

Because my wife and I are a couple who work in unity in the hard times, our unity when life is good is over the top.

Ecclesiastes 4:12 –*"Though one may be overpowered, two can defend themselves. A cord of three strands is not quickly broken."*

- Have you ever faked your way through hard times?

- Can you sit and listen and validate your spouse's feelings without judgment?

- Do you and your spouse have a common goal to be united together in all areas of your lives?

- What action steps will you take to achieve that unity?

Prayer: Lord, I pray for your guidance and direction in becoming united with my spouse. Like Ecclesiastes 4:12 says** - "Though one may be overpowered, two can defend themselves. A cord of three strands is not quickly broken." **Lord, let my

spouse and myself be united with you to create a chord of three strands that cannot be broken. In Jesus name – Amen.

Victim no More

Romans 8:37

"No, in all these things we are more than conquerors through him who loved us."

When I walked into my first meeting of alcoholics anonymous (AA), I heard these words from an old timers mouth – *If you're drinking because of him, her, it or any other person place or thing, you'll never quit drinking.* Something about those words intrigued me and I contemplated them for the next two days. When I saw the old timer again, I asked him what he meant by the above statement. He said to me, *Randy, if you're drinking because you're a victim, you'll never quit drinking.* Those words were exactly what I needed to hear. You see for the thirty-plus years before walking into the rooms of AA, I was living my life like a victim.

The reality is that I was and always will be a victim of abuse. The difference is today I don't live my life as a victim. I would tell my wife that until she had walked in my shoes, she had no right to tell me what to do. I would tell her and others that if what happened to me happened to them, they'd be drinking and acting this way as well.

So long as I was drinking and using, it was impossible to get out of the victim role. So long as I was drinking and using, I was delusional about what was causing my pain, and I was in total denial about my responsibility to others and myself. So long as I was drinking and using, every problem was someone else's fault. After all, I justified to myself, how could my problems be my fault?

To heal, I had to get clean and sober. There was no more evading or denying that truth. I had to deal with my childhood, and I couldn't do that while I was still drinking alcohol and taking drugs. My marriage was on the line, but I had come to realize over the year of therapy that my very *life* was on the line, too. It was time to surrender to God and the process of recovery.

Psalms 147:3 – *"He heals the brokenhearted and binds up their wounds."*

- Are you still harboring anger towards something or someone from your past?

- Are you now ready to release that anger and give it to God?

- What action steps will you take to release your anger?

Prayer: Lord, remove the anger that has me trapped and replace it with your love and give me the strength to forgive anyone that caused me pain. In Jesus name – Amen.

Weeds or Flowers

Deuteronomy 22:9

"You shall not sow your vineyard with two kinds of seed, or all the produce of the seed which you have sown and the increase of the vineyard will become defiled."

When I first met Cathy, I was constantly tilling the freshly planted garden with love by the way I treated her. She was my queen, and I wanted her to know it without reservation. I spoke words of kindness and love as well as buying her gifts such as flowers and jewelry. I was planting the true flowers of love in her heart and in no time, those seeds blossomed into a love that I never imagined possible for a guy like me.

Over time, however, the seeds of love that had been so delicately planted and cared for began getting choked out. The roots of my unresolved childhood issues had never been uprooted. Those weeds had only been mowed down by the love that Cathy had shown me and continued to show me. My drinking increased, the weight of the world became too much for me, and the woman that I had fallen in love with and married, suddenly was not good enough for me. My constant badgering of her to take better care of herself, better care of me, wore her down. Slowly, and over time, the weeds of my unresolved childhood issues started to choke out all the flowers that Cathy and I had planted in our garden over time. Cathy's love for me was fading, as it should have. After all, I was no longer tilling and fertilizing the soil of our garden with kind words or loving actions.

After ten-plus years of recovery and recommitting our lives to Christ, most of the roots from my childhood trauma have been removed from my garden, and Cathy has done her own root pulling. Today, our garden is filled with nothing but the fragrant smell of flowers of love. Yes, now and then a weed that we missed pops up. However, when it does, we immediately recognize it and take the time to dig up the root of the weed that is trying to choke out our love for each other.

Are you pulling up the roots of the weeds that are trying to choke out your love for your spouse, or are you just mowing the grass with shallow apologies?

Hosea 10:12 says – *Sow righteousness for yourselves, reap the fruit of unfailing love, and break up your unplowed ground; for it is time to seek the LORD until he comes and showers his righteousness on you.*

- Is your garden filled with the sweet, fragrant smell of the flowers of love?

- Is the sweet, fragrant smell of the flowers of love being choked out by the weeds in your garden?

- Are you just mowing the grass or are you pulling the roots of the weeds in your garden?

Prayer: Lord, I pray that you give me the courage and strength to dig up the roots of bitterness, anger, hate, resentment, and un-forgiveness. I pray that you replace the roots of bitterness with sweetness, hate with love, and resentment with friendliness and un-forgiveness with the roots of forgiveness. In Jesus name – Amen.

We do Think Differently

Genesis 1:27

"God created man in His own image, in the image of God He created him; male and female He created them."

There is no doubt in my mind that Cathy and I think differently and I thank God for that. If the two of us thought the same, our marriage would be a disaster. In many ways, we balance each other out and in many ways we frustrate each other, but we would not have it any other way.

Speaking for myself, without Cathy in my life, I would likely have more enemies than friends. I tend to draw hard lines in the sand about certain topics in life, and over time, I have learned to talk with Cathy when I feel like I'm getting ready to draw one of those lines. Cathy knows my heart and how passionate I am about helping others in recovery. She can also see where my passion can hinder my logic. She never persuades me from the outcome I am working on; she only gives me another way to look at it, thus making my approach much more loving and compassionate. All of which results in a much better outcome.

Except for my book or when I am preparing a teaching, Cathy has read all of my college papers, blog writings and the devotionals I am writing prior to me submitting them. Again she looks at things differently and sees things from a different perspective. I'm not looking for her to change the content of my writings nor does she want to. However, because I am so emotionally attached to my writings, I often will complicate the issue I am writing about. Cathy looks at it with no emotions, more like an everyday reader, and gives me ideas to make my writings more reader friendly. Again, the result of which is not changed, but often better.

The downside to our different thinking was also the cause of lots of pain in our life. When I was at the peak of my disease, Cathy lost herself and her voice. Because of my anger and rage that reared its ugly head at the most inopportune times, Cathy

63

would not tell me to quit drinking. She actually partied with me out of the fear of how I would react if she were to say no. Thank God that all came to an end over ten years ago. I am happy to say that Cathy has her voice back and I honor that voice.

If you are married or in a serious relationship, remember your spouse is not you. Honor the fact they think differently than you and figure out how to capitalize on their strengths. Remember your spouse is your *partner*, and not your *enemy*.

Genesis 1:28 – "*Then the* LORD *God said, "It is not good that the man should be alone; I will make him a helper fit for him."*

- In what ways are you and your spouse different?

- Do you compliment your spouse with your differences?

- Do you allow your spouse to make loving and complimentary suggestions to you?

- What action steps are you going to take to allow your spouse to feed into you in a positive manner?

Lord, help me to be open to seeing the differences between my spouse and myself as a positive thing. Help to ask her for opinion or view on things, as I tend to be pretty black and white in my view of things. Help me to humbly receive my spouse suggestions as a gift, not a threat. In Jesus name – Amen.

What God Has Put Together – Let No Man Tear Apart

Mark 10:9

"Therefore what God has joined together, let no one separate."

Cathy and I have been married for over thirty years now and we have had more than our fair share of struggles. I can tell you that the only reason we are still together today is because God was always present in our lives. Does that mean we were always going to church, being of service to others and living a God-centered life? Absolutely not! If God is everything or he is nothing, and for me he is everything, then he is the one responsible for Cathy and I being together.

From the first day I met Cathy, I knew there was something special about her. Her outer beauty was only enhanced by her gentle spirit and inner beauty. God knew exactly what I needed in a wife when he put Cathy in my life. I have always told people that if there were angels on earth, Cathy was the one God gave to me. I could not have asked for anything else in a woman; she was everything I had ever dreamed of.

Somewhere along the journey, I became discontented and started trying to change Cathy, mold her into something she wasn't. My unresolved childhood issues, the ones I thought would magically disappear when I married Cathy, started rearing their ugly head. My depression, anxiety, alcohol and drug addiction and discontent set in. I did not feel I deserved a woman like Cathy. How could anyone love me the way she loved me, it just wasn't right in my eyes.

We had every possible distraction thrown at us. I became emotionally abusive towards the woman of my dreams, alcoholic, and even had an affair, which can be one of the most damaging things done to a woman. Yet, Cathy remained true to her vows. She knew the real Randy was still inside and did not want to give up on him. Instead, she chose to ask God for help and fight for her marriage and I am so grateful she did.

Marriage is not easy, and sometimes it requires hard, painful work. It can seem easier just to walk away and start over with someone else. The only problem with that is, the problem you had with your last relationship will only show up in your new relationship. Why, because wherever you go, the problem follows. You can't run from yourself, which is where the real problem lies. Instead of running, stand firm on your vows and work through all your issues together. I promise you it will only draw the two of you closer together.

Remember husbands and wives, your spouses are your partner and helpmate, not your slave.

Ephesians 5:22 says – *"Wives, submit yourselves to your own husbands as you do to the Lord."*

However, men don't get all excited, as there is a prerequisite to our wives submitting to us.

Ephesians 5:25 says – *"For husbands, this means love your wives, just as Christ loved the church. He gave up his life for her."*

The second greatest commandment is to Love Your Neighbor as You Love Yourself and your spouse is a neighbor.

- Are you treating your spouse like a slave or like a partner and helpmate?

- Can you look at yourself in the mirror and say that you *really* love yourself?

- Do you love your spouse as you love yourself?

- What does that look like?

- What action steps are you willing to take to really and truly start loving yourself and your spouse?

66

Prayer: Lord, I ask that you open my heart and eyes and show me the ways I can start loving myself as you love me. In doing so, I will see where I have not really loved my spouse the way I am instructed to according to the word. As I begin to love my self, let my love grow for my spouse and theirs for me. Your will be done, not mine. In Jesus name – Amen.

www.ingramcontent.com/pod-product-compliance
Lightning Source LLC
Chambersburg PA
CBHW032029040426
42448CB00006B/777